As Autumn Fades
by
J.T.Wheeling

Black Leaf Publishing
www.blackleafpublishing.com

ISBN 978-1-907407-35-2

THE BLACK LEAF PUBLISHING GROUP
83 Clipstone Rd West
Forest Town, Mansfield
NG190ED
Nottinghamshire
England
www.blackleafpublishing.com

Dedication:

I dedicate this miscellaneous collection of verses to my grandsons. In time they may even come to appreciate some of them.

Due to the increasing pace of technological innovation, the gap between the generations has never been wider, but what has not changed is human nature. Youngsters today still have to deal with the challenges all past generation faced.

The oldies' perennial cry of "I wish I had known when I was young the things I know now!" is one reason why we old folk wish to pass on such wisdom as we may have accumulated to those whom we love and cherish I wish also to dedicate this to all of "Tomorrow's Generation", those young people of today, whose inheritance is our planet Earth with all of its wonders and challenges. There are, as always, many problems, but with courage, persistence and love, they can build a better world.

Invitation to the Reader

Walk with me
Down the long canyons of the years,
Take this winding way from fears,
The joys and tears of youthful indiscretion,
Confusing depths, to heights of inspiration.

Come with me,
Seek the path that leads to mountains,
Leave the rich lands, golden fountains,
Find the cleaner air, the valley's secret wynd,
Green cloaked by oak and ash and pine.

Join with me,
Ignore the ageing back, the legs that tire
As we ascend our path, and so up higher
Towards the peak, austere against the blue,
Onwards together, always me—and you.

Fly with me
Beyond this vale of flesh and trial, to where,
Ethereal in another realm of purer air,
Exultant spirits sing, enjoined and free to rest
In that shining place, where all are blessed.

May 2010

As Autumn Fades

Sections:

Wanderers

Martial Matters

Contemplations

Old Memories

My Native Land

Magic

Seasons

Young Folk

Elements

Wanderers

Gypsy

The village was our home then, with ripening fields of corn,
Bright memories of childhood, the place where I was born,
We children played together, rose early with the morn,
And then we saw the stranger come walking from the dawn.

He travelled from the mountains along the river's side,
His clothes were long and dusty, his hat was dark and wide.
Great tales he brought to thrill us, but long he could not bide,
We begged for more, he shook his head, and then at last replied.

"The elf-land horns are a-calling me from very far away,
My restless spirit hears them, I know I cannot stay,
The evening star now glimmers to guide me on my way,
Tomorrow shall not know me; long gone by break of day."

Mist Walker

He walked in mists of mountain moor,
He breathed the chilling air
And knew that times had turned again,
For all the fields lay bare.

Within his heart the certain song,
Within his soul the cry
That soon the time would also come
When he must leave this sky.

Another home would welcome him
With all his old loved friends,
With ancient woes dissolved in time:
That great realm never ends.

His shadow had outlived its time
Would darken ground no more;
His fading path led to that gate
The way to evermore.

North Wind to the Pilgrim

Where I pass
Silvered grass
To catch from far
The Northern star
Whose light was old
Ere tales were told
Or we were born
On distant morn.
My touch is cold
To men grown old
With growing loads
On weary roads.
"Despair", I say,
"Of finding day.
On my white bed
Lay down your head!"
But duty trains,
Refutes, constrains
My siren song;
And men march long
Night hours away
Towards the day
With hope a flame
And Christ a name.

Passage through Danger

He walked the ways of moonlight glades
And heard the pipes of faery chime
Their haunting notes to charm the soul
Of mortals held by strands of time.

Entranced he wandered far among
The guardians of that silvery realm,
Their names recalled from early years,
Oak and beech and ash and elm.

Dark shadows all around they stood
Reaching for the star bound sky,
Afraid to stop, he knew the tale
If mortal stops he soon shall die.

So up the paths he climbed alone
And came to where the hill stood bare,
Far off and high, on mountains pale,
The gates of dawn now opened there.

The paling stars, their message sung,
The fading moon, her magic fled,
As eastern skies began to blush
With dawn's first kiss of fiery red.

Now birdsong echoes, mountain song,
And winds of life began to stray,
He took great breaths of freedom's air,
And faced the challenge of his day.

Pied Piper

He passed through strange and curious ways,
And witnessed many acts of man
And marvelled at their folly.
But then he joined the careless throng,
Forgetting hills and seasons' songs,
The sound of waters rolling.
Be-dazzled by the cities' lights
And artificial pleasure,
Where raucous bands do blind the ear
To music sweet and tender.
He learned to fight with harder hands
And push ahead of others.

I met him on a wintry day,
His brilliance was amazing,
My problem solved, I thanked him well
The years that followed darkened.
(We seldom value what we have,
Till it is lost forever).
With tricks to charm and words to spin,
All snares to catch his prey,
He used them well, then went his way
But never looked behind him.
A smiling front, though blood behind,
Ahead—admiring fellows.

Yet in the darkness one survived,
For looking back I saw the wreck
Of all that lay behind him,
I cut the link and turned away
Returned to things of yore:
True friends, and love at home.

Johnnie Come Home

Old stars as sharp as knifes are out,
The wind it breathes to kill,
White water swift has daggers grown,
And every bird is still.

Soldier, sailor, travellers all
The bitter truth must learn,
Who flee from all the early joys
For evermore must yearn.

The vanished years are seen by change
Their passage marked its way,
And kinder now are stars of night
Than brutal light of day.

Alone this night in bitter wind,
The prodigal he stands
Apart from all the things he loved,
An alien in his lands.

Traveller

I have known the wind
And the distant ways it goes,
Far from here.

I have heard the stars
Their ancient silvery laughter,
Far from here.

I have seen the glory
Bless that land we love,
Far from here.

I have loved my friends
In that lost and distant land,
Far from here.

Stars and wind and love and glory,
Realms and times of former days,
Wait perhaps, after this story,
Restored in ways beyond our ken.

Vagabond

Dazed by the dance of the raggle-edged leaves
And tumbling birds in the sky,
Westward I turn my wearying steps
For shelter, ere day should die.

Summer long gone, now autumn and storm
Rain from a darkening sky,
Rest from a vagabond's wandering ways,
A roof, and a place to lie.

Far in these mountains, I remember it well!
There's a cave that's deep and dry,
Secure from those white signs of sleep,
Dread gifts from a wintry sky.

Climbing those paths in the teeth of the wind,
Stumbling still on my way,
With fire in my heart and a goal to win,
Ere night can swallow the day.

Beach Stroller

Golden fires of the dying day
Far to westward wend their way.
Alone, alone on the wave-washed sand
I print my steps, then turn to land.

Rugged and dark the line of the hills,
Silvered and kissed by mark of the rills,
Away and beyond, the first evening star,
A faint ancient light that has travelled afar.

A lad conceived, begotten and born,
A soul from the depths of times forlorn:
My spirit returns once more to acquire
Its worldly burden of flesh and desire

That bright western fire yet touches my soul
With visions of wonder beyond man's control,
A promise of glory in realms that lie far,
Sealed by the light of that distant star.

Martial Ways

Soldier's Return

Look now, children, here he comes
With muted trumpets, silent drums,
Up the wandering forest ways,
Home from war's long bloody days.

Nights to come of haunted dreams,
Sounds of pain and human screams,
Winds lamenting at his door
For friends now lost, for evermore.

Wearied years behind him lie,
Times of torment, hearts that cry
Life laid waste in far-off lands,
Duty done—but stain-ed hands.

From seeds of battles, widely sown,
Come bitter harvests, swiftly grown;
These riches all will come to you
Heritage you may not eschew.

Night Roving

This night I lie awake and hear
The far-off thunder of the waves
A hundred miles from here:
So far—and yet so near!

So near—and yet so far
I smell that ocean's air,
Beyond the mountains' bars
Asleep beneath the stars.

I also know the heart of those
Who serve in other lands
Below the crackling gun
Brave lads, and all so young.

A bullwork, as our mountains are
Against the storms the world brings.
They hold our honour high
Below the sun, beneath the sky.

The Old Patriot

In the dark night that covers our land
Honour is a distant, nameless star.
For the wind comes out on a storm filled night
To blow the stars away,
Their ancient light is hidden from sight;
Memories only stay.

The ways of our land are tattered and strewn
The spirit of Empire torn
Rags of that glory, ancient and fine,
Blow in these storms forlorn.
Forlorn, forsaken, forgotten and bare,
Changed by lies and scorn,

Suckled on envy, raised to despair
Vision bereft, unsworn.
Where shall our children seek their stars,
How shall they find their way?
Parasite bled, with cynical scars,
Leaderless, lost, astray.

Lives there no one with heart to inspire,
With faith and vision to fill
This chasm of night, rekindle desire,
Arouse our ancient will?
Stir up our purpose, rise and reform,
Blazen the way again!

Last Post

Tendrils of sad wind creep through
These crevices of door and sill,
Moans of disembodied hunger haunt
My dreams, this endless night.

Madness stalked this town, now little stands,
All friends are silent now.
Within this pit of fear, alone
I bare my teeth, await the foe;

'Defend your land'—ancestral cries—
From a far corridor of time.
Tattered and torn our flag now lies
Begrimed by blood and pain.

Once, here the childrens' laughter rang,
While traders plied their wares,
To dusty travellers on their way.
Then some mad priest harangued the throng,

With ancient passions roused the fires.
'Your God demands you give your lives...'
I hunger still for truth, some place to stand:
To rip this cancer from mankind.

When young, I heard another call,
'Your God requires,' My question hangs,
'How many fearsome gods are there?
'What, only one—then who has heard aright?'

You priests, who order death and pain,
Destroy the work of our Creator,

Who built with love—and only love
Then gave us all freewill.

You claim His ear to maim and kill?
Deluded fools, be dumb for evermore!
Now, nearing dawn, my time has come
My song and life have bled away,

In times to come they'll find my bones,
Last soldier in a town long dead.
I leave these words to make their way.
To better times and brighter day.

Lament

Gone are the leaves on a weeping wind,
November calls in the river's roar,
Regiments gone with the dying year,
Who are now left to care?

Pipes and drums lie gathering dust,
Music long past on the air;
Silent for now is the marching of feet,
Our soldiers who went to war.

Tradition and honour have crumbled away,
Like blood of the long vanished men,
Valorous tales--mere dust on the wind--
For pygmies now rule our sad land.

November 2004

Commonwealth Heritage

In foreign fields the fallen lie
Buried deep where they did die,
Such far-off land with blood they named
As old Britannia's, dearly claimed.

Names, sons, traditions,-bitter pills
Washed down with tears and drowned by time,
Memoried now on carved stone,
Or unmarked grave, apart, alone.

Empire's gains are lost and gone
So what is left to call our own?
Greece left culture burning bright
In hearts of scholars through the night,

Rome left cities, laws and ways,
A treasure house for later days
Then Europe woke and fiercely filled
The girdled world in which to build.

Such far-off lands acquired by blood
Gave their own lives to stand as free.
These ancient deaths are mingled now,
Are one in dust that winds still blow.

Grown now beyond our national claims
One world we have to share
Together in the years to come,
And make old Earth a better home.

From Cordoba

For every lad the bugles call,
For every lass the tears
For lover gone, to stand or fall,
Among the smoke of wars.

The reason why is seldom plain,
The truth is wrapped in lies,
Power-mad men demand your pain-
Too quietly speak the wise.

Tolerance once in ancient times
Among these gardens flowered,
As wisdom came from East to West
Great benediction showered.

After Armageddon

The broken spears of evening
Have pierced the storm-wrecked sky;
All tumbled down in bloody pain
This last lorn day shall die.

For none shall wake to praise the dawn,
Not one be here to know
If out the coming, blackest night,
Bright morning winds will blow.

The breaking spears of maddened men
Have soared, have sought, have won;
Their purpose done, our world is gone,
The death-clouds linger on.

So who shall count the paling stars
While waiting light of dawn,
And who shall love this cindered world
When all the men are gone?

Why?

*"It is nothing to do with me or with you,
It is faint, it is far, it is gone!"*

*I am sure that it called, it drummed and it beat,
The sound of the marching of millions of feet.*

*"But it is nothing to do with me or with you,
It is far, it will pass, it will die!"*

*Yet I know that I heard, I know that I cared,
We are free, they are not and will die.*

*"It is very far away in a land we do not know,
So why should we bother now or care?"*

*We see the eyes of children
Brimming brightly with despair,
What hope is for our world
If we fail to reach out there?*

Contemplations

Conjecture

Before matter
Before time
Nothing was.
Then—a Thought!
And magnificence
Was born.
Now we stand
Aware,
Below
A trillion stars.
First Thought,
Then matter,
Then us
To think.

So ask
Whence came
That Great Thought
And why?

A Distant Music

O song that hides within my heart,
And night by night must sing its part,
From dust and rain this body strong,
A prison for my restless song.

This dust round others once did twine,
Each atom is as old as time;
But that which sings within my soul
Does not know time—and never will!

From far they came, and further, far
Beyond this Earth, beyond our star
A place that is not bound by years
And knows not hurt, nor loss, nor tears.

A memory is left of music fine
From that far place, remote, divine,
The source of that which blesses me,
And by its singing sets me free.

This gift the ancients left behind
These fierce regrets can bring to mind,
For only those who hear it know
The distant lands to which they go.

Spirit Song

(Many heroes die unsung, unremembered even by their peers.)

Not in the haunting of the winter moon,
The song of thrush or plaint of loon,
Nor in the singing of a child at noon,
Do the wonders of this world appear.

Search not for glory in the tumbling skies,
Ablaze with colour when the long day dies,
Drummed by surf-song and the seabirds' cries,
The wonders of this world are not in these.

Seek not these wonders in the power of men,
The kiss of brush, the lyric lilt of pen,
The transient works that briefly entertain,
Such wonders of this world do not remain.

The wonders of this world are not in these
Not wind in forest, nor starlight on the seas
Not song, nor laughter, neither hope or ease
The wonders of this world are none of these.

But- Hear the music in a deaf child's heart,
Sense the colours when poor eyes have failed,
Feel the striving in a lame man's gait,
And marvel at the spirit's triumph there.

Behind the silence of a dead one's eyes,
Unbarred and still, an empty prison lies;
Free, and far with friends, the battling spirit flies-
Another wonder to this world dies.

Sea Parable

And though his name is known no more
His spirit aye does haunt that shore
Which braves the great Atlantic storms.

The seethe and surge of waters then
Inspires our valiant fishermen
Who brave the great Atlantic's storms.

The rocks that bind our stalwart land
'Spite wind and wave, do still withstand,
These grey-washed skies and driving storms

He walked this beach 'er I was born,
He knew the loss of ships forlorn
That bowed before Atlantic storms.

Though all now born shall one day die
Our blood is strong, with spirits high
We shall defy this life of storms

50

Gone Away

When brightness to the skies has flown
And my shadow haunts the ground no more,
Seek my wandering in the starry spaces
That mark our expectations on this shore.

Silence brings the music of the spheres,
Whose splintered light sets all bright colours free,
Benediction falls when all else fails,
Drowned lands, and ancient fables of the sea.

Candleflame lights sanctuaries of the soul,
Absence wakes memories of better time.
And, as light of vanished stars still burn,
The tyrannies of time are slain by rhyme.

O'er ancient times before our years began
The veil is drawn, no memories remain,
Yet still a haunting music pleads its cause
And wakes the genes within each pulsing vein.

Night Song

The song before the last was best of all,
Night-lost between the sea-wind and the moon,
Star-bright it soared aloft and captured all our hearts,
A haunting melody, whose magic failed too soon.

Alone we come, then, for a while, together
Celebrate the brightness of our time,
Gild fleeting hours with hopes for glory,
Recalling tales in tramp of rhyme.

We never see how swift the moment passes,
Companions gone leave only silent chairs;
Night's fires all fail and dawn brings only ashes,
Such are life's sweet and sour affairs.

After Epiphany

Out of the wilderness I come,
Filled with the light of Eternity,
Returned to ancient friends.
But where is the 'I' who went a-wandering
In the wild ways of the world,
Nigh sixty years gone by?
Gone, gone utterly,
No ego shell remains:
Only a raindrop back to ocean.
Again I am a wind returning,
Redolent with breath of that vast sea
A clarion call from distant realms.
Oh smell the ocean, breathe its airs,
Hear my songs with open hearts,
They are for all mankind.
Know each and every spirit
Is but a blossom on that
One universal tree, the source for all.
Now let your spirit sing its truth aloud
To guide your ways;
And let the ego fade unheard.

Separation

I—alone,
You—alone,
We alone,
Souls singing
From a cage of bone.
Hear my song
Then sing to me
Of the time
We'll all be free.
Once together.
Long ago
Filled with love
Afar from woe
Then transition
Into time
And forgetting
Things divine
But look forward
Hope's a-rising
Beyond these trials
A new horizon.

Cassandra

Alas, I am Cassandra
Sad prophet of these days,
Ignored by rushing fellows
Too busy on their ways,
Who chase the transient pleasures
And worship earthly treasures,
Consumed by great ambition
They waste the passing days,
They do not heed my warning
Nor hear their bound souls sighing.
Forgot lie times of summer
When freedom's song was king
Alas, Cassandra's burden,
It bears me to the ground,
While mad folk dance so wildly
I sing, without a sound.
Unheard my gentle weeping,
Unnoticed on my way,
For all I love is passing,
For it has had its day.

Anti-Rap

If all of the singers of songs,
Who brighten the ends of our days,
Forget to honour the notes
And muddle the words of their praise,

Then faster shall fail our evenings
And darker our hearts shall grow.
For discord breeds fear and confusion
And nonsense brings chaos, we know.

Yet weapons we have now a-plenty
To hold back the gloom of the night,
For melody brightens our darkness
And returns us the use of our sight;

The rhythm of rhyme shall revive us,
As joyfulness wakes in the song,
True notes evoke a rare beauty
Of love, till morning is born.

Time

1

Parted by more than distance, few do understand
It's light that bears all time away
'Prisoned in its golden bars.
Lift up your head and count the stars
-Yet know they are not there-
They moved on many a year ago.
And some whose light doth grace this night
Were dead 'ere you were born
You do not see the here and now,
You watch the vanished years,
As light that bears all time away
Preserves it in its bars.
All time is round you, then and now,
A cocktail of the years.
And even as the storm clouds pass
The greater sea of stars blaze forth
To set you free of time, in time,
Because your time is now.
Whatever fires within you burn
Still let your light shine forth:
Nor hesitation stop, nor any fear'
Prevent your life from shining here,
That ever more your soul shall live,
Alive in light's bright bars.

Time

Do not forget by night or day,
Nor in the storms that ride the sky,
Nor in the sun that blinds your eyes,
That ever, ever burn these stars
Whose light holds time within their bars
The time that bears your life away
Memories may last awhile,
As candles in the fleeting hours
Illumine life in rooms around;
But know their light shall fail you soon;
Light, held by time, cannot survive,
Time, held by light, shall ever shine.
Be patient, oh my restless ones,
Count not the passing hours,
Awake through light to prisoned time;
Perceiving this, your life springs free
To everywhere and every time-
Do not forget the stars!

Evensongs

1

This time of glimmering beauty holds all within its spell,
Those sacred hours of twilight when nature holds her breath
While hushed fields grow harvest's gold, 'er winter brings his
death.

The northern light still shimmers on, a memory of day,
Quiet hills around stand shadow tall against the turquoise sky,
And weary hearts at last knows rest and are prepared to die.

Such times of tranquil peace are few and far between,
Yet benediction for the heart, a glimpse of future heaven
Beyond the strife of greedy men, remote from grief and pain,

2

Ashes of the burning day lie smouldering in the west,
Ambition joins that pyre, old times when dreams were best,
Reality of dark rolls in to drown all in the night,
Yet high above, remote and far, the stars still send their light.

3

Beyond the darkening waters, a girl's sweet voice is heard,
Entranced the people listen, their hearts with her are shared.
The notes of such clear singing bring joy to all who hear,
An angel's song below the stars, it wings across the mere.

Old Memories

Impermanence

*Stand on your isle of wind and storm
And read the truth the waves do form,
Relentless pounding salty spray
Shall eat our hard land's heart away.*

*Across the wide and fertile lands
Nothing built forever stands,
E'en mountains, old in years, shall be
By rivers bourne to distant sea.*

*Our spirits bound to time in wed
Shall leave their flesh on dying bed,
Inexorably flow the paths of time:
Escape it on these lines of rhyme.*

Adieu.

Yes, we all must go, off to the distant lands.
You have left in this the loveliest of autumns,
Land laden with gold that time shall also take
Soon, when wild winds come; leaving us
To wait awhile and find our way
Towards a different ending.
All things pass into another joining,
Sorrow should not cloud our joy
At this your fresh beginning.

The Girl from Home long since has Flown.

Child of the loving, giving heart,
With life and laughter free,
As mist around the morning star-
That girl is far from me.

Age shall not wither the light of her eyes
Nor dim the joy of her days,
Winds of the wild once carried her songs
And rivers mirrored her ways.

Lost to the wiles of innocent youth
Deaf to all cries of alarm
Drowned in the torrents of ancient joy-
Wounds for the heart forlorn.

Cry on the shore of sundering seas,
Weep for the child that is far.
Gaze at the grey sky, pray for a sign-
That mist on the morning star?

For Jussi

Old songs before the day's declining ends,
Lost sounds before the last light dies;
One voice recalls the glory Heaven lends
And hails its passing on the evening skies

Colour fails as roses scent the air,
Stillness reigns while ancient stars appear,
Memory stirs, yet still the voice is there,
Gentle, sweet, a friend to every listening ear.

Plaintive, pleading, with power to rouse the soul,
Then fading, that fine-spun source of sound
He sings to you, your heart strings aye respond,
But nevermore its likeness shall be found.

September 1960

For Tim

Friends do fall from life and die,
As colours fail the darkening sky.
Then stars appear, remote but bright
As memories shine, they stay to guide
Bereft companions through the night.

They pass from life of wine and song,
On shadowed paths are swiftly gone.
Their laughter echoes down the wynd.
'Ere time shall shade them from our ken,
Companions leave their friends behind.

28th September 1994.

Before and After

Before the wind, before the mountain,
Before the ocean's ancient roar,
Remote in space and far off time,
The burning of the stars was there.

When Earth's a cinder, empty, old,
And all the seas have gone to air,
And all the air has blown away,
Those stars shall trek their endless trail.

And where shall you and I be then,
Einstein, Plato- everyone
Who've shared this fleeting, spinning home,
Before our planet's time was done?

Be comforted, be comforted,
And know that at the end
Of this perplexing twist of years
There stands a radiant friend;

Beyond, there blows a garden
That shines with blossomed love,
Each seed you sowed with kindness,
Each one for whom you cared.

They stand in welcome greeting,
They guard with patient minds,
The mysteries of our living,
Till all of us come home.

Winds of Time

Day dies, its memory stains the heaven,
Stars call, their light from long ago,
Darkness seizes all in his possession-
I feel the winds of time along my bones.

Friends leave and go about their calling,
Strangers come, and do not understand,
Loved ones go to cross the paths of dying-
I hear the notes of time along my bones.

Wars sound and cull the best from living,
All people pass and ancient nations fail,
Life goes, then after all have fallen-
The notes of time play tunes among their bones.

My Native Land

Banished

There's a rising wind 'lo the moon tonight,
The clouds are scattered and torn,
He travels alone, with eye still bright,
Though mission lies lost and forlorn.

Here in the wind and rocketing rain,
Sun on the mountains high,
Heir to these lands, ancient of name,
A Prince on the Isle of Skye!

Charlie's the lad, now vanished and gone,
Still mellowed by myth and years,
Forgotten the havoc long left behind,
The blood, the deaths and the tears.

Exile's Song

There was an island
Spun between dawn and sunset
Heaven and ocean,
Mountain starred, sea-struck, and-
Beautiful.

Lit with a luminosity of air
Fragrant, heather proud, fair,
Far fable famed,
Long loved in song, in memory held-
Beautiful.

Storm-stern, mysterious,
Ghosted by the ancient races,
Mist enchanted,
Mountain crowned, high forest ferned, and-
Beautiful.

There was an island,
Ancient, winged, proud,
Hebridean aired,
Cuillin heart so beautiful, yet-
Gone.

Lone Highland Lands

Tales of the Clearances haunt us all still,
Ghosts in the glens, strange tracks on the hill,
Gone are our people to Canada bound,
Australia, New Zealand and other far ground

Vanished the clansmen, banished and gone,
Still honoured in spirit, remembered in song.
Great was their sorrow, yet spirit stayed strong,
They are our legend and legends stay long.

Those blue rugged mountains that edge the far sky,
Still hold the echoes of breaking hearts' cry
Cursing the landlords, those heartless hard men
Expelling their people for money and gain.

Chorus
Now isles of dawn and sunset, that brave the western sea
Call out across the oceans, 'O come you back to me,
To glens of haunting beauty, to mountains high and free
My waterfalls and rivers, I hold them just for thee!'

Anthem

Amidst a waste of misty seas
A mountain vastness stands,
Her granite heart defies the storms,
Her children all are free.

With spirits clear as mountain peaks,
Though scattered to far lands,
Their heads and hearts with pride arise,
When Scotland's name commands.

Infused by light, the colours change
And visions come and go;
Enriched by such ephemeral fire,
Her children's souls do grow.

A prisoner on the binding staff
Her tattered flag still flies,
A symbol proud, yet glory's gone,
The wounded legend dies.

Like all our fine ambitions
Exposed to wind and years,
An ancient tatterdemalion
Our colours still it bears.

Yet honour is more than a word,
Our heritage bold is centuries old,
Your name is bound to your pride,
Scotland the Brave is our fame!

So up, my lads, to the mountain
Defy the wind and the rain,
The world lies waiting and ready,
Awaken the nation again!

Caledonian Songs

1

Land of mist and rugged mountain,
Land of the highland men,
Beloved in song and rich in story
Bless-ed are by sun and rain.

Driven from here our sons were scattered
At the world's far ends they roam,
Yet ever at night, when the music's alight,
Our singing shall bring them home.

Men from the lowlands, men from the cities,
Men from the border hills,
All know the secret, strong in their hearts,
Wakes, when the pipe song thrills.

Often repressed, yet never defeated,
Staunch in our faith are we;
Fair stand our mountains, bright are our rivers,
Wild rolls our guardian sea.

Chorus
Estranged cousins, far and lonely,
Wandering on your world-wide way,
Listen! Listen! Faint and fading,
Pipes are calling, far away:
"Scattered sons of Caledonia
Let us call you home today".

95

Heads forget, though hearts remember,
Yearns for what you do not know,
"Return, return," your blood still whispers,
"To ancient home, beloved, far,
Where mist enchants the sea-cast mountain,
And nightly calls the northern star".
City-bound you fret and struggle,
Acquiring weight of worldly wares.
Tears of time and seasons' glories
Slip behind you as you know
The cataract of life roar onward
Unrelenting, on its way.
Remember stars are bright above you,
Hidden only by the day.
Priceless hold the years you're granted
Spend them fully on your way.

Chorus
Estranged cousins, far and lonely,
Travelling on your worldly way,
Stop and listen, faint and fading,
Pipes are calling, far away:
"Wandering sons of Caledonia,
Let us call you home today".

Magic.

Brightness.

There is still a brightness there
Shimmering in the evening air;
Quick! Before such glory dies,
Hold the truth within your eyes,

That your friends bemused in dark
Illumined be by divine spark
Lightning strikes but now and then
Catch the moment, Damn the pain!

None believe, the moment gone,
The power that was extinct, goes on
Yet such truth within us burns,
Guides our going, marks our turns.

Recognised by friends and foes
Strikes them new, then onward goes.
Quick! before such glory dies,
Catch the truth within your eyes.

Faerie Song

Awake O mortal from your dream,
And leave your friends forlorn,
Arise to dance among the stars
Until the flush of morn!

You'll not forget my elfin notes
In all the times that be,
Through all the witless waste of years
When you shall not be free.

So listen, listen long my lad
When autumn stars stand cold,
And now and then you'll hear a note
From faerie times of old.

Do not forget, all down the years,
The music of our song
Which star and wind and forest sing,
That you may know your own-

Your own and secret singing self
Which none may shade nor mar,
And from your being let it shine
With gladness like a star.

With music, laughter, love and friends
To fight the world's woe,
As winter storms transform the dark
With magic shining snow.

Sundown

Whenever you leave the tumult
And climb a beckoning hill,
At the magic hour of sunset
When even the winds are still;

With luck you may discover
-If you listen with heart and mind-
The ancient consolations
That are there for all mankind.

They lie there waiting forever,
They shine like the evening star,
But loud roars the course of living,
And ever the truth seems far.

Beyond the grasp of the greedy,
It hides from the glare of sun,
But open your heart at evening
When tumult and noise are done.

The dreams of the day are illusions
That mask the march of the stars;
Awake to the meanings that matter,
Unlock the gates of your bars.

So turn from the grasping fever,
Seek not 'mong earthly things,
The glory that lives forever,
Is found in the heart that sings.

Eternal Walker

He walked the painted evening,
His rags to glory torn,
His trail gave birth to magic,
As early stars were born.

Sun took his slow departure,
Winds sang their old refrain
That ever man shall suffer,
While moons shall wax and wane.

He walked the painted morning,
And wept to see the world
A dustbin of the broken
Where many lives had failed.

Time treads its solemn measure
Of centuries and hours,
And ever these were squandered,
Except by youth and flowers.

For they remember glory,
Expect it to remain
Despite his passing footsteps,
His gifts of loss and pain.

But we, the wise and lonely,
Forget that early song,
And misuse all our talents,
And know not right from wrong.

He walks our painted evening,
His magic is still there;
But only you can find it,
For others do not dare.

Greater Ocean

Beware, aware the nights that flare,
The millioned windowed sky;
The little lights, those pinpoints bright,
They wheel, but do not die.

For they will steal away the hearts
And souls of mortal men;
They stand beyond more gates of time
Than we may comprehend.

Our ocean's beat may call our fleet,
And we can sail away.
That sea of time's beyond our sail,
Earthbound we now must stay.

Yet nightly still they burn and call ,
So strong our spirits yearn
On wings to rise beyond this sky
Those starry ways to learn.

The Call

Still the road can lead to Faerie,
Somewhere faint and far away,
Seek the ancient vanished places,
Secrets distant as yon star
Glimmering in the winter skies.

Down the ways of wind and water,
Leave the sheltering trees alone,
Farewells said to friends and kindred
Dwindle on the airs behind;
Hunt for wilder lands beyond.

Hidden at the source of rivers,
Buried in the mountains' bones,
Scent of ancient things still lingers,
Primeval prints of what has gone,
Preserved alone in tale and song.

Come and find us in the mountains,
Misty glens disguise our lair,
Music's magic holds our password,
Pipes keep calling, come away
Find us at the close of day.

Thoughts

My land is full of spirits
That sing their songs to me,
Beyond the clutch of ticking time
Their realm is bright and free.

Then there are the darker ones
Who whisper of desire
Of lust for all that Earth can bring
And all you may acquire.

Now we may choose to listen
Or send such thoughts away
For always they are tempting
To lead our steps astray.

Free choice we have while living
But know that spirits sing
And listen to the brighter ones
As all around they wing.

Seasons

Hawthorns

October's winds now blow again,
The river's high with gift of rain,
I watch the brown leaves flowing by
Old glory gone. they now must die..

The slanting rays of evening's light
Now kiss the waters shining bright,
The river's song brings peace to me
As on it rolls to distant sea.

The high slopes' ranks of standing pine
In shades of green the hills do line,
While lower down the failing light
And thickening air, foretell the night.

Yet, red amongst the darker green
Bright hawthorns make their presence seen,
A memory's glimpse of summer sun,
A warming touch, when day is done.

Old Country Song

The stars they blossomed brightly,
The sheaves they stood so still,
We climbed the path that led us,
Up old October hill.

Remember, oh my darling,
The moon above the mill,
The river turned to silver
By old October hill.

That serenade of beauty
Of nightingales' sweet trill,
The perfumed air of autumn,
Round old October hill.

Recall how sweet the loving
Across the years e'en still,
The magic of that blessing
On old October hill.

Northern Summer

Far and high in the luminous air
The glimmering light lives on,
The wind has torn the clouds apart,
The stars are yet unborn.

Midnight has come, and memoried sun
Still pales our Northern sky,
This is the hour the minstrels knew
Old tales that never die.

And Beauty, Beauty guards the gate,
Where glory paves the way,
And music gifts her wings to souls
Who yearn to fly away

Beyond the mud, the noise and pain,
Beyond the wearying years
Whose lot is loss, whose word farewell,
Whose gifts are dust and tears.

Yet Beauty's smile shall ope' the gate
And music set us free,
So drown-ed spirit's breath returns
To likes of you and me.

This magic night's elegiac hour
Shows distant stars afire,
Melodic airs' resplendent tones
Of voice and lute and lyre.

September

September days are best of all
The time when all the leaves do fall
And carpet lawns in bronze and gold
A sign the year is growing old.

In early autumn's star-strung night
When air stands still and moon grows bright
The clearer skies bring cold so dire
That, kissed by frost, the trees catch fire

September's winds awake my heart
From summer's dreams it's time to part,
For storms shall come to strip the trees
And winds will dance with dying leaves.

September's songs bring harvests home,
And bees are robbed of honeycomb,
The orchards yield the summer's reign
And fields are bright with golden grain

Green October

A blaze of sun, a morning cold,
A dust of snow from ice-blue sky,
The trees still mazed in green and gold-
October shall not die!

Remembrance soon for memories old,
Of sacrifice by those who lie
In far off graves, their story told-
October shall not die!

This summer came and went again,
A misery taste of stricken hell,
An endless dirge of wind-cold rain,
Till golden Autumn spun her spell.

Deep burnished fires have seized the wood,
White gulls now scour the sky,
I watch the raging colours brood-
October shall not die!

October 1985

Autumn

Here are-

Words written that have found no home,
Thoughts thought that, elusive, roam
And drift like phantom ships, to ever stray,
Forbidden harbour by a tide that cannot stay.

There are-

Leaves fallen that still spell their story,
A forest mantel tapestried with glory,
Bird-song under Autumn's skies
A tale each Spring brings new, each Winter dies.

And I-

In memory for the fallen years,
Stand idly by and watch those leaves
Reaped by storm from lonely trees,
Lorn letters on this leaden sky
Writ by wind, go flowing by.

1969

127

Winter Welcome

Aye, and now that Winter comes, forget October's sun,
Tie down the stacks, call in the kyne, for here the storms shall run.
Already heralds ride the sky: last night I watched awhile,
A freezing hour, in bitter wind, as Winter came in style .

He cast his fingers down the air and clothed the heights in grey,
He blew the colours from the air and took the light away,
He strung the chains of cackling geese across the marbled sky,
And stripped the leaves from beech and ash, bereft, alone to die.

He called his knights from out the East, bediamond-ed with stars,
He mocked the moon with planets bright, great Jupiter and Mars,
And snared the sun in reddening mist, to wander blind along
The icy ways of skeletal trees, to only cold wind's song.

And we who know how seasons flow, swift as seconds gone,
Feel Winter's kiss along our bones, and wander on forlorn.
The anger of despoiled Earth now comes in flood and storm,
No refuge now for futile Man, no shelter deep and warm.

December 1990

Question

Engrossed by tales of autumn,
Bright scripted by the leaves,
A multi coloured maelstrom
Among the gathered sheaves,
Engrossed in contemplation,
A whirlpool of dreams,
Where nothing is quite certain--
I wonder what it means.

Answer

It means that winter is coming
With blizzard and cleansing rain
Preparing land for the blessing
When springtime comes again.
It means our world is turning
And spinning around its sun,
A part of continual creation,
Our home since time has begun.

Young Folk

Poetry is the bridge between the 'reality' of the physical world and the magical realms of romance and imagination. This bridge takes us over the river of time, by which we are all confined, and leads to places where anything is possible. Poetry is more than halfway to music, that language of the Gods which nourishes our very souls. For both poetry and music speak to the heart, the centre of all emotion, and emotions form the seas through which our spirits have to swim. So give our children the rhythm of rhyme: it is a lifetime gift.

A Childrens' Song

Leaves of crimson, leaves of gold,
Show the year is growing old,
Soon November's mists shall rise,
Mysterious lands and haunted skies.

December brings back Christmas joys,
Time of parties, childrens' toys,
Carol singing, Christian birth,
Jesus born for all the Earth.

Salvation promised down the years,
End of sorrow, end of tears.
Love the Godhead, love the key,
Only love can set us free.

An Old Stone Carving

There you stand, here lie I
Underneath the self same sky;
Once I was before your time
And carved these words in stone and rhyme.

Those circling stars so far above
Know naught at all of human love;
Their very light proceeds our time
Which give these thoughts to carve in rhyme.

This ancient stone can thus be seen
Transformed into a time machine,
A one-way message crossing time,
Bourne far on wings of stone and rhyme.

City Kids

Come walk the fields of autumn, recall the vanished days,
The redolent fields of summer, and hidden leafy ways.
The birds, whose calling echoes and tell us to arise.
Hear river's song at evening, when colour leaves the skies.

You stalk the streets of cities and breathe the smoky air
The seasons pass unheeded, make little presence there,
And nights do not bring darkness, for yellow lights do glare,
While transports roar unending and raucous speakers blare.

Awake, you banished children, and claim your old birthright
To see the hills at morning and bathe in rivers bright.
And when the evening darkens, just watch the wakening star,
And see your home the Universe, that reaches—oh so far!

Your heart shall sing with wonder, brimful of rising joy,
This treasure-house of nature, remembered as a boy.
So leave the buildings gloomy, the artificial ways,
Turn those footsteps homeward, and live in better days.

Christening Prayer

May-
Love and the stars shine upon you,

May-
The winds and waters of this world welcome you

May-
The benedictions of fellowship lighten all your days

May-
All your talents bloom and flower,

May-
Your spirit find sanctuary at departure.

I pray.

Rain

The winds across the oceans blow
And drink to fill the air,
So form the mighty thunder clouds
That bring our water here.

The rain it falls from clouds above
To bless our land below,
And when at last the storm has passed
The crops do thrive and grow.

The rivers on the mountain feed
And bring them, grain by grain
Back to the source whence all has come,
The mothering seas, again.

I look upon your laughing face,
Bright spirit come from heaven,
And wonder what you'll carry home
When all your years are given.

I also see the millions born
To pestilence and pain,
Their pleading eyes, their hungry hands,
Their need for blessed rain.

Nails and Wood

Some years ago a child was born
Who grew to love the world,
By nails and wood he learned his trade
And taught his friends with word and deed,

And, showing them love for all mankind,
He gave them supper ere his end.
By nails and wood he found his death
That love might save the world.

Elements

Dark Angels' Passing

Again the Great Ones walk the land,
Bringers of a greater storm;
They flatten fields, they pluck the trees
And scatter tales of distant seas.

At night they roam the hills and moors,
Occluding stars and sailing moon,
They mutter at each door and sill
Demanding more, and never still.

My sleeping heart is roused by them,
I raise my head, I smell their airs,
I hear their song and sense their way
And know that nothing here can stay.

As sad as lovers forced to part,
Or slow as mountains feed the sea,
All things must soon or later pass
As swift as leaves across the grass.

Again the Great Ones stride the land,
With Pentecostal firing wind
To touch with light each wandering soul,
Transforming all to clean and whole.

Harbingers of the Day

Quiet waking emblems of the dawn
On far horizons clear are drawn,
Above the mountain's golden crown,
Fresh rising light the stars shall drown,

While coming day its splendour sounds
With trumps of glory, joy propounds.
Bird songs now grace the morning air,
A haunting sound beyond compare,

From high the mountain torrent leaps
Torn white by wind. The icy peaks
Resplendent now with golden glow,
Promise heights to which we go.

Storm Song

I carry the scend of the far-away seas
On the wings of my roaring air.
I shred the gold from old autumn's trees,
And leave them skeleton bare.

Rivers run fast with the weight of my tears
They carry my fury away.
I've raged round Earth for all of my years
Yet restless, I never can stay.

Clouds mask the sun, obscuring the stars
I darken your nights and days,
So cower in your beds or drink in your bars,
Till, laughing, I've gone on my way.

From tropical seas I replenish my power,
My castles I'll build in high air,
Then realms of your lands I shall again scour
And leave them all barren and bare.

Eagle's Song

*From distant heights where hides my home
I soar the airy wastes alone,
In search of prey the skies I roam
The lands beneath, dark earth and stone.*

*When dawn's first kiss on eastern peaks
Proclaims the colours of the day,
My chicks awake with hungry beaks
And send me hunting on my way.*

*The lilac skies stretch all around,
The airs are quiet, the lakes are still,
Long shadows reach across the ground,
I spy my prey and make the kill.*

Hours

It is the hour of dawning,
The hour the cockerel cries,
Dispelling night with rising light,
The time when all arise.

It is the hour of noontime
And high triumphant sun,
With shadows short, a-drip with sweat,
The work of man is done.

It is the hour of evening,
Blue heavens gently transmute
To burning gold, then birthing stars
The wears of day confute.

It is the hour of midnight,
The heavens stand tall, revealed,
An everlasting song of stars
Wherein our hurt is healed.

Each hour holds forth its blessing,
Time's stations rolling by
Towards our destination
Of glory in the sky.

Wind Song

Oh dance of free air that men call the wind,
To feather the clouds and freshen the land.
Write your swift tunes on waters once still,
Waltz with the trees and tell me your tale.

Once you were cradled in far distant realm,
Nursed by old starlight, then woken by sun
Who sent you soaring, the oceans to roam
Building air castles of mists and seafoam.

You strip all the trees when autumn has come
And roar in the forest with thunderous drum,
When blizzards and storm bring snow metres deep,
You lull all the land through winter's long sleep.

And then in the springtime you waken the land
Commanding the seeds to sprout forth and stand
Bright green the leaves that now dress all the trees
You murmur of summer, of blue skies and seas

The Tidal Bell

Majestic breakers thunder on the broken rocky shore,
With fury unabated they rise again for more.
White gulls scroll their tapestry across the wind blown sky,
Screech their wild excitement with loud and raucous cry.

The tidal bell is clanging its old and mournful sound,
The fishermen are ready, now leaving westward bound.
Ashore I stand 'lone watching, long gazing out to sea,
My weary heart is aching, no sailing days for me.

The waves have cast their blessing, the scend of angry sea,
It rises to the headland where my cottage shelters me.
There I dream remembrance, the brighter times of old
When we, a band of brothers, were bright and strong and bold.

Yet each day still its treasures bring, to lift a lonely heart,
Old hunters' moon spins silver tales, as starlight plays its part,
So, dreaming by the ocean, my spirit does restore
Its deep and strong defences, that stand forever more.

This morning's benediction, a quiet and pale scrubbed sky,
Hears calls from men returning, not one had gone to die,
The widow making weather had mercy shown at last,
The ocean stilled its anger, the winds their icy blast.

Tonight the boys will greet me and tell their salty tales
Of shoals of silver herring, and porpoises and whales.
We'll sing the songs of fishermen until the night turns grey,
And up the headland we shall climb, to greet the shining day.

11th Feb 2010

Silence

Grief has no voice,
No words to speak of loss,
Of hearts struck empty,
Left hanging on a cross.

Letters spell all words,
A vocabulary of desolation,
Yet grief has no ears
To hear of consolation.

The axe has struck
Its paralysing blow
And grief is dumb
Is all we can know.

Do not ask why,
Reason cannot reply,
Time's healing wings,
Stilled, no longer fly.

Hour-long seconds crawl
Around the wounded one.
Yet 'morrow is a foreign land
Where grief may find a tongue.

An Ending

You are waiting, I am watching,
Stars go drifting on the wind,
Time's forgotten years are fading,
I but turn—and they are gone,
Ancient dreams and drowning passion,
All once dear, have fled away.
Night, once splendid, falls submissive,
Greets the banners of the dawn.

Lightning Source UK Ltd.
Milton Keynes UK
171976UK00001B/4/P

9 781907 407352